David Hume

A

LETTER

FROM A GENTLEMAN

to his friend in Edinburgh

(1745)

Edited by
ERNEST C. MOSSNER & JOHN V. PRICE
for the University Press
EDINBURGH

MCMLXVII

85224 003 1
Printed in Great Britain
at the Curwen Press

*
⁖⁖⁖

Acknowledgments

Permission to publish this pamphlet by David Hume was granted by the Trustees of the National Library of Scotland. The editors are particularly indebted to its officers: William Beattie, Librarian; J. H. Loudon, Keeper of Printed Books; and Robert Donaldson, Assistant Keeper. They take pleasure in returning thanks to several other scholars who have also provided generous assistance: Miss Helen Armet, Keeper of the Burgh Records, Edinburgh; George Davie, Charles P. Finlayson, and D. B. Horn of Edinburgh University; William Maclagan and David Raphael of Glasgow University; and Ian Ross of the University of British Columbia.

E. C. M. J. V. P.
Edinburgh
22. vi. 1967

Table of Contents

Introduction

        The most prominent British philosophers of the mid-1740s as viewed from the present day were Bishop Berkeley, Francis Hutcheson and David Hume. Of these, Berkeley was past his philosophical prime and in his 'tar-water' phase; Hutcheson was Professor of Moral Philosophy at Glasgow University, the 'never-to-be-forgotten' teacher that Adam Smith was to commemorate; and Hume, the youngest and most brilliant, was virtually unknown. To be sure, Hume had published three volumes of *A Treatise of Human Nature* (1739–40), an *Abstract of a Treatise of Human Nature* (1740), and two volumes of *Essays, Moral and Political* (1741–2)—all of them anonymously. The *Treatise* was generally ignored, and the *Abstract* was so ephemeral that it dropped out of sight until the present century; only the *Essays* enjoyed a modest success.[1]

        Younger son of the laird of Ninewells in Berwickshire, Hume would have welcomed a respectable post to supplement his small inheritance and to make possible what he so ardently sought, to lead the life of letters. The chair of Ethics and Pneumatical Philosophy at Edinburgh University, soon to fall vacant, met Hume's requirements. His candidacy proved unsuccessful, and the pamphlet printed here in facsimile, *A Letter from a Gentleman*, was written as one move in a campaign of hope and despair. Little known elsewhere, the young Scottish philosopher, in the event, was but too well known in his native city—and by the wrong people.

I. The chair of Ethics and Pneumatical Philosophy (popularly, and later officially, known as 'Moral Philosophy') was held by Dr John Pringle (1707–82), who had been elected in 1734. However, he had been on leave since 1742 to serve as physician to the army, and in the spring of 1744 was appointed Physician-General to HM Forces in Flanders. In a letter of 20 June 1744 N.S., to John Coutts, Lord Provost of Edinburgh, Pringle offered to resign so that a successor might be chosen. Provost Coutts suggested to his young friend, David Hume, that he apply for the post. The Provost would have a considerable voice in the election to come, because the University was a civic foundation and the Town Council chose the professors. Hume was willing, and at this stage everything seemed propitious, as he gaily informed William Mure of Caldwell: 'Mr Couts . . . desir'd me to mention myself as a Candidate to all my Friends, not with a View of solliciting or making Interest, but in order to get the Public Voice on my Side, that he might with the more Assurance employ his Interest in my Behalf. I accordingly did so; & being allow'd to make use of the Provost's Name, I found presently that I shou'd have the whole Council on my Side, & that indeed I shou'd have no Antagonist'. [2]

But professors are not wont to give up their chairs easily, and the evidence which filtered in to Provost Coutts and the Town Council of Edinburgh indicated that, in reality, Pringle did not wish to resign but was angling for an extension of his leave of absence for yet another year. This the Council were unwilling to permit, and they instructed Coutts to request Pringle either to return by 1 November 1744 or to resign immediately. Wishing to avoid offending Pringle, however, the Council sanctioned ambiguous wording, which Pringle seized upon to continue equivocating. For months Pringle managed to avoid committing himself and succeeded in committing the Council to even further deliberations and ultimatums.[3] November had arrived, classes had begun, Pringle had not returned, the chair had not been declared vacant, and much of the urgency to appoint a professor had dissipated. Pringle's students continued to be taught by two substitutes, one of whom was eventually to get the chair—William Cleghorn (1718–54).

On 27 March 1745, nine months after Pringle's original letter of June 1744 intimating resignation, his actual letter of resignation was received by the Town Council. (Miscast as professor of philosophy, Pringle was to earn lasting fame for his study of diseases of the army; he later became President of the Royal Society.) Now a successor had to be chosen. Now Hume came to realize that his chances were considerably less than they had formerly been. Not without some ironic appreciation of his position, he wrote to a friend, 'that such a popular Clamour has been raisd against me in Edinburgh, on account of Scepticism, Heterodoxy & other hard Names, which confound the ignorant, that my Friends find some Difficulty, in working out the Point of my Professorship, which once appear'd so easy. Did I need a Testimonial for my Orthodoxy', he continued playfully, 'I should certainly appeal to you. For you know that I always imitated Job's Friends, & defended the Cause of Providence when [you] attackt it, on account of the Headachs you felt after a Deba[uch]'. Setting playfulness aside, Hume then called for help: 'But as a more particular Explication of that particular seems superfluous I shall only apply to you, for a Renewal of your good Offices with your Nephew Lord Tinwal, whose Interest with [John] Yetts [3rd Bailie with special responsibility for the University] & [Thomas] Allan [Dean of Guild] may be of Service to me. There is no time to lose. . . . A word to the wise' (*HL*, 1, 59-60). Even as Hume wrote this letter to Matthew Sharpe of Hoddam, on 25 April, his cause had been pretty clearly lost. Nevertheless, it indicates that Hume remained hopeful and the outcome unpredictable.

As a matter of fact the Town Council, in the absence of

some of Hume's supporters on 3 April, had already seized the opportunity to elect a professor. They chose a man whose eminence was undoubted and whose abilities Hume admired, the Professor of Moral Philosophy at Glasgow University, Francis Hutcheson (who curiously appears in the Council minutes as 'George Hutchison'). No doubt this choice raised ambivalent feelings in Hume. On the one hand, Hutcheson was among the few philosophers in Britain whose philosophical proclivities were even remotely similar to his, and Hume cites him in this connection in *A Letter from a Gentleman* (30). Moreover, Hutcheson and Hume had corresponded about some philosophical problems raised in Book III of the *Treatise*, 'Of Morals', which Hutcheson had read in manuscript and for which he was willing to provide his own publisher, Longman. On the other hand, Hutcheson had opposed Hume as a choice for the Edinburgh chair on the grounds that he was 'a very unfit Person for such an Office'. Hume found this notion 'absolutely incredible'. 'All my Friends think', he had lamented to William Mure of Caldwell as early as 4 August 1744, 'that he has been rendering me bad Offices to the utmost of his Power. And I know, that Mr Couts, to whom I said rashly, that I thought I coud depend upon Mr Hutcheson's Friendship & Recommendation; I say, Mr Couts now speaks of that Professor rather as my Enemy than as my Friend. What can be the Meaning of this Conduct in that celebrated & benevolent Moralist, I cannot imagine' (*HL*, 1, 58). Small consolation to know now that Hutcheson had not expressed his adverse opinion out of self-interest: he was never a declared candidate and declined to accept the chair when it was presented to him. Hutcheson deemed Hume unfit for the Edinburgh chair presumably because the University Senate had imposed on the holder of the chair at the time of Pringle's election in 1734 the duty of reconciling Moral Philosophy with Divinity. In particular, the Professor was directed to prælect every Monday 'upon the Truth of the Christian religion'.

I I. Although Hutcheson's refusal, in theory, made it still possible for Hume to be elected, the opponents leagued against him—the majority of the Ministers of Edinburgh, who had supported Hutcheson, and others of a political cast—were too strong for Hume or, for that matter, for any candidate proposed by Provost Coutts. Political factors, indeed, had become paramount. The Principal Secretary of State for Scotland in Pelham's administration was John Hay, 4th Marquess of Tweeddale, first appointed in 1742 in Lord Wilmington's administration, after Walpole had been forced to resign. Tweeddale was the leader of the 'Squadrone Volante', a third force operating between the Argyll-Islay interest and the Jacobites. The office of Secretary of State for Scotland, which had been revived for him, placed in Tweeddale's hands tremendous powers of patronage: 'Thus Tweeddale got the control of Scotch affairs and very ill he managed them'.[4] His political career as Secretary was short-lived. Charged by the Argyll interest in 1746 with showing weakness toward the Jacobites and making no provision for the emergency of the 1745 'invasion', he was driven out of office and the Secretaryship itself was again abolished. Nevertheless, early in 1745, he was greatly interested in the proceedings of the Town Council of Edinburgh and, as the final battle over the professorship drew near, was receiving almost daily reports from various 'informers'.

The Town Council were divided on issues other than the election of Pringle's successor, and the divisions found Provost Coutts and his adherents on the one side and the Tweeddale allies on the opposing side. There had been, for example, a skirmish over the choice of a Collector of Supply for the city. So one of Tweeddale's informers, Alexander Arbuthnott, could write, on 23 May 1745: 'The next tryall of Skill amongst them will be the Election of a prophessor of morall philosophy, which I hope will also go against them, att Least no pains Shall be neglected to make it go So. I am att present very well with those in the opposition as they Imparted to me Every Step of their management without reserve and they had any Little assistance I was capable to give them. Sir John Inglis is of great Service as he has Severall in the Councill that regard him very much'.[5] In a letter of the same date, Thomas Hay, kinsman to Tweeddale, wrote to say that Coutts had been defeated in the matter of the Collector of Supply, and that 'I hope he will likewise be foiled about the Professor of moral Philosophy & in all appearance he will'. Much of the opposition to Hume, it seems, was in reality opposition to Coutts and his party, and political intrigue worked against Hume even more adversely than the charges of 'Heresy, Deism, Scepticism, Atheism &c &c &c.' that he complained about to Mure of Caldwell.

The issue of the vacant chair was basically part of the power confrontation between the party of Coutts and the party of Tweeddale. On 26 May, Thomas Hay observed that 'Deacon Cuming had declared he was under promise to Lord Elibank to vote for Mr Home because his Lordship had got a Brother of Cumings recommended in the fleet & Mr Arbuthnot said that all he believed it would be practicable to bring Cuming to would be to be absent'. Like all laymen concerned, Hay viewed the election in a purely political light, but he was not without a certain ironic awareness of the effect Hume's 'Heresy' and 'Atheism' were presumably having on his friends and supporters. 'I hardly think', he opined, 'that any politic consideration has led Lord Elibank to draw Cuming off. I presume he has meddled out of friendship to Mr Hume for My Lord & he [Cumin] & Provost Couts are all too wise to enter into the vulgar mistakes of Christianity'. Had he known it, Hume could hardly have failed to appreciate that sally. But others than Cumin were being influenced by the hope of 'good deeds', continued Hay. And he explicitly stated what was at issue, so far as the Tweeddale camp were concerned: 'Couts's party have all the opportunitys of availing themselves of the effect of power. There is little of that on the other side which will be the great drawback till your Lordship Stand on a better footing. But I don't mean by this that your name is mentioned or that you are even suspected to know any thing of this matter'. While a modern reader may find it curious that Tweeddale would be so deeply concerned about the appointment of a professor of Moral Philosophy, as master of government patronage in Scotland the Marquess could make his power felt in every area of national life and did so to secure his interest.

III. The final election was scheduled to take place on 29 May but it was postponed. Before this event and about the middle of May, twelve of the fifteen Ministers of Edinburgh at a joint session with the Town Council had given their *avisamentum* (the exact legal status of which is uncertain) against Hume. The three ministers in the minority were Patrick Cumin, Professor of Church History at Edinburgh University; Alexander Webster, minister of the Tolbooth Church; and Robert Wallace. Moderator of the General Assembly in 1743, Wallace was the most liberal Scottish churchman of his time, and one of the many Moderate clerics whose intelligence and conversation Hume appreciated. Hume's gratitude to Wallace on the occasion of the *avisamentum* was fairly expressed: 'I think Mr Wallace's Conduct has been very noble & generous; & I am much oblig'd to him'.[6]

As might be expected, Thomas Hay had no appreciation of Wallace's liberal view of Hume. In a letter of 1 June, he wrote: 'Mr Wallace seems to have mistaken his politics in this case more than his brother Mr Cuming has done. And as for Provost Couts, that he may defeat Mr Cleghorns party at any rate, He has yesternight offered his interest to Principal Wishart whose friends are now laying themselves out for it & yet it is not many days since the Principal & Mr Couts were at Great variance publickly'. Clearly, Coutts, in turning to Wishart as an alternative candidate, was not exclusively interested in the election of Hume. He was set for the defeat of Cleghorn, certainly not because of Cleghorn's doctrines of moral philosophy (of which in all probability he had no knowledge), but because Cleghorn was the candidate of the challenging opposition. This same letter of Hay indicates that the suspicions of the Edinburgh clergy entertained by Coutts were also those of Hume: 'Provost Couts was pleased to say in the meeting this week that he believed that most of the Clergy who gave their avisamentum against Mr Hume had never read the pamphlets whence people had taken a bad impression of him...'. One of those present, according to Hay, thought the accusation 'impertinent' and said so. When it was suggested that he appeared to be in a passion while making the charge, he replied 'that he really was not & would again repeat it cooly & thought So'. Apparently no attempt was made to ascertain who had read what.

Yet that very question demands investigation. Exactly what was Coutts referring to when speaking about 'the pamphlets whence people had taken a bad impression' of Hume? To judge from the title-page and opening sections of Hume's own pamphlet, *A Letter from a Gentleman*, one is almost compelled to believe that it was called forth by an earlier pamphlet (or just conceivably a manuscript) written against him. Quite likely this putative pamphlet was entitled (with possible minor variants): 'A Specimen of the Principles concerning Religion and Morality, maintain'd in a Book lately publish'd, intituled, *A Treatise of Human Nature*, &c'. This 'title' from Hume's title-page (with an italicized 'said to be' here omitted) is repeated in full in the first sentence of his 'Letter' with the addition: 'being an Attempt to introduce the Experimental Method of Reasoning into Moral Subjects', thus completing the title and sub-title of the *Treatise*. Hume announces that he has read the *Specimen* and also 'what is called *the Sum of the Charge*', describing them as 'Papers' which his 'friend' (Coutts) informed him 'have been industriously spread about' (1). Further on, Hume writes of the '*Specimen* and *Charge*, as transmitted to me' (18). This *Sum* or *Summary* 'is intended, I suppose', Hume surmises, 'to contain the Substance of the whole' (19); if so, it was probably appended to the *Specimen* itself. Possibly, it might be argued that there were two distinct 'papers' or pamphlets directed against him. Indeed, Coutts's remark, quoted by Hay, might imply that there were several pamphlets, perhaps both for and against Hume, but a careful search has failed to reveal any other documents bearing directly on the election. At any rate, it is clear that this appointment was exciting rather more attention than the usual appointment of a professor to a university.

One of those most adamantly opposed to Hume's candidacy was the Reverend William Wishart, *secundus*, Principal of Edinburgh University, 1737–54. He had been elected by the Town Council on 10 November 1736 but was not inducted until 9 November 1737. Oddly enough, during this interim, Wishart found himself in serious trouble for alleged heresy, being charged by the Presbytery of Edinburgh with having published two sermons that contained sentiments contrary to the doctrines of the Church of Scotland. (He did not sufficiently stress the importance of original sin.) Several pamphlets were written for and against him, and in 1739 as an aftermath to his eventual acquittal, Wishart published *The Principals of Liberty of Conscience Stated and Defended; In a Letter to a Friend*, under the pseudonym of 'GWITMARPSCHEL-DON'.[7] In it, he observed: 'I frankly own to you, that I look upon all use of Force or Punishment in the Affairs of Conscience or Religion, considered *as such*, to be an infringement of the natural and unalienable Rights of Mankind; inconsistent with the proper Office and Duty of the Civil Magistrate; contrary to, and subversive of, the Nature of true Religion; and peculiarly opposite to the Spirit and Genius of Christianity: I cannot but reckon it the natural right of every Man to enquire and judge for himself in the Affairs of Religion . . .' (3-4). If nothing else, Hume, had he known of Wishart's declaration of faith six years before, could have found a sufficient example in that clergyman to justify his own pamphlet.

IV. As it was, Hume was convinced that Principal Wishart

was his chief antagonist among the clergy and the man primarily responsible for his defeat. Indeed, it is safe to say that *A Letter from a Gentleman* was provoked by a pamphlet (or pamphlets) by Wishart against Hume. In dealing with the accusations against him, Hume was unquestionably reading from a specific document and quoting from it verbatim in the opening two sections of his pamphlet. The marginal numbers are references to pages in the *Treatise*. Many of the quotations from it are abridged or altered or otherwise mutilated. The first is Englished from the Latin of Tacitus into 'Rare Happiness of our Times, that you may think as you will, and speak as you think'. Whereas the *Treatise* reads, 'I am first affrighted and confounded with that forelorn solitude, in which I am plac'd in my philosophy, and fancy myself some strange uncouth monster, who not being able to mingle and unite in society, has been expell'd all human commerce, and left utterly abandon'd and disconsolate' (1.iv.7)—words with a peculiarly ironic ring in 1745—the 'quotation' in *A Letter from a Gentleman* is reduced to, 'I am confounded with that forlorn Solitude, in which I am placed in my Philosophy' (4).

To take one of many other examples, on page 12 of *A Letter from a Gentleman*, the *Treatise* is quoted as asserting, on page 280 of the first volume, that '"This Opinion [about the Deity as prime mover of the universe] is certainly very curious, but it will appear superfluous to examine it in this Place".' The *Treatise* (1.iii.14) reads as follows: 'This opinion is certainly very curious, and well worth our attention; but 'twill appear superfluous to examine it in this place, if we reflect a moment on our present purpose in taking notice of it. We have establish'd it as a principle, that as all ideas are deriv'd from impressions, or from precedent *perceptions*, 'tis impossible we can have any idea of power and efficacy, unless some instances can be produc'd, wherein this power *is perceiv'd* to exert itself'.

One further sample of Wishart's malicious citations

from the *Treatise* will suffice to demonstrate his desire to make Hume appear unduly hostile to religion. It is worth repeating here because it is one that haunted Hume throughout life. The *Treatise* is made to read (10), 'That *any Thing* may produce *any Thing*; Creation, Annihilation, Motion, Reason, Volition; all these may arise from one another, or from any other Object we can imagine', a sentence which is then labelled a 'curious *Nostrum*'. In context, the passage from the *Treatise* (1.iii.15) actually reads as follows: 'According to the precedent doctrine, there are no objects, which by the mere survey, without consulting experience, we can determine to be the causes of any other; and no objects, which we can certainly determine in the same manner not to be the causes. Any thing may produce any thing. Creation, annihilation, motion, reason, volition; all these may arise from one another, or from any other object we can imagine. Nor will this appear strange, if we compare two principles explain'd above, *that the constant conjunction of objects determines their causation*, and *that properly speaking, no objects are contrary to each other, but existence and non-existence*. Where objects are not contrary, nothing hinders them from having that constant conjunction, on which the relation of cause and effect totally depends'. It is only the deliberate omission of 'without consulting experience' that makes the following sentence a 'curious *Nostrum*'.

Towards the end of *A Letter from a Gentleman*, Hume declares, 'and you know how easy it is, by broken and partial citations, to pervert any Discourse, much more one of so abstract a Nature, where it is difficult, or almost impossible, to justify one's self to the Publick. The words which have been carefully pickt out from a large Volume will no doubt have a dangerous Aspect to careless Readers . . .' (33-34). Hume himself was driven to reconstruct his ideas in the *Treatise* from memory rather than from the *Treatise* itself. 'I am sorry', he acknowledges, 'I should be obliged to cite from my Memory, and cannot mention Page and Chapter so accurately as the

Accuser. I came hither by Post and brought no Books along with me and cannot now provide myself in the Country with the Book referred to' (32-33). When he composed *A Letter from a Gentleman*, Hume had taken up his duties at Weldehall, near St Albans, Hertfordshire, as tutor to the 'mad' Marquess of Annandale. Lacking a copy of the *Treatise* and having only a document allegedly quoting from it, he wrote a reply, noting with great understatement that the anonymous author's selection of quotations, 'these *maim'd Excerpts*', did not accurately represent his published ideas.

When Hume learned that he had been defeated in his bid for the professorship, he wrote to Henry Home (later, Lord Kames), who had published *A Letter from a Gentleman* on 21 May without authorization: 'I am sorry you shou'd have found yourself oblig'd to print the Letter I wrote to Mr Couts, it being so hastily compos'd that I scarce had time to revise it. Indeed the Charge was so weak, that it did not require much time to answer it, if the Matter had been to be judg'd by Reason. The Principal found himself reduc'd to this Dilemma; either to draw Heresies from my Principles by Inferences & Deductions, which he knew wou'd never do with the Ministers & Town Council. Or if he made use of my Words, he must pervert them & misrepresent them in the grossest way in the World. This last Expedient he chose, with much Prudence but very little Honesty' (*NHL*, 15). The use of the word 'pervert' immediately catches one's eye, as it is part of the same charge Hume makes in *A Letter from a Gentleman* (33).

V. The letters to Lord Tweeddale concerning the Edinburgh professorship of Moral Philosophy confirm that at the last meeting of the Town Council in which Hume was irrevocably defeated no one was really sure what the outcome would be. Thomas Hay had written on 4 June, the day before the meeting, to say that 'Mr Arbuthnot is in hopes that Mr Cleghorn may still prevail notwithstanding the junction betwixt Provost Couts & Principal Wishart'.

This is in reference to Hay's observation of 1 June that Coutts, if he could not ensure the election of Hume, was willing to join forces with one opponent in order to defeat another. Both Coutts and Wishart, though hardly on friendly terms, were of the Argyll interest and united in opposition to Tweeddale. The Principal, whose salary as such was negligible, may have been willing to step down to a somewhat more remunerative professorship. If elected, he could hardly have held both posts for very long. Yet, as Wishart came from a wealthy and well-connected family, it is more likely that the political issue was dominant.

The persistent opposition to Cleghorn on the part of Coutts and Wishart was certainly intensified by the fact that the Cleghorn family were well entrenched ecclesiastically and politically. Cleghorn's mother was Jean Hamilton, daughter of the Reverend William Hamilton, who was Principal of Edinburgh University, 1730–2. She had three brothers, Robert, Gilbert and Gavin. Robert Hamilton, a Minister of Edinburgh, doubtless 'played an important part in the advice of the ministers of Edinburgh in regard to the vacant chair'.[8] Gilbert Hamilton was a minister of Cramond on the outskirts of Edinburgh. Gavin Hamilton, the bookseller (who in 1754 was to publish the first volume of Hume's *History of England*), was an influential member of the Town Council. Thus Cleghorn had two uncles, one in the Church, the other on the Council, pressing his candidacy. He also had the backing of the Tweeddale party.

This final meeting of the Town Council to decide on Pringle's successor was held on 5 June 1745. The following day Alexander Arbuthnott told Tweeddale the good news of Cleghorn's election. Yet it was not so much the election of Cleghorn as a person that caused the rejoicing of the Tweeddale party as it was the fact, so neatly stated by Arbuthnott, that 'our friends have prevailed in getting Mr Cleghorn appointed'. Coutts's shifting strategy in the affair of the professorship is thus detailed by Arbuthnott: 'the man Mr Coutts first Sett up was Mr Home a Son of

Ninewalls; when he found that he could not carry him then Mr Law whose father [William] had formerly been prophessor [1708–29] was Sett up and when that could not be brought to bear as his Last Shift, he Sett up principall Wishart, though he by no means Liked the man, yett he judged him the only person that could defeat his opposers and therefor Sett him up but yesterday when the affair came to be determined he had only twelve of the Councill for him and Mr Cleghorn had nineteen. . . '. Arbuthnott exults: 'this affair has made some noise in this place, which makes the victory the more remarkable'. And he concludes by advising that the important thing now was for the opponents of the present Provost Stewart and the late Provost Coutts to unite in order to prevent them from retaining power and control. Also writing on the day after the election of Cleghorn, Thomas Hay is even more forthright: 'I fancy Provost Couts's party is broken & after the two late overthrows it may be less difficult to defeat him than it has been hitherto'.

Though a man of some importance as the founder of a great banking dynasty, Coutts displayed little parliamentary or political skill. Twice a bailie, he entered the Town Council in 1730 and was elected Provost in 1742, a post he held for two years; he was succeeded by Archibald Stewart, another friend of Hume's. As Provost, Coutts attained at least one real distinction: 'He is said to be the first provost to entertain strangers in his own house instead of in taverns at the town's expense'.[9] There is no record that Hume knew of Coutts's desperate last-minute substitutions of Law and Wishart in the election campaign, but he was not a little vexed over the Provost's handling of his candidacy. Writing in that sense to Henry Home, the philosopher also showed a due regard for Coutts's efforts on his behalf: 'I am as little surpriz'd as I am vext at the Turn this Affair has taken. I have indeed a great Regard as well as Sense of Gratitude for Mr Couts, & am heartily sorry he shou'd have been defeated by a Pack of Scoundrels, tho it was entirely by his own Fault' (*NHL*, 16–17).

VI. In the light of our knowledge of the machinations of over a year, the bland notice appearing in both the *Edinburgh Evening Courant* and *The Caledonian Mercury* of Thursday, 6 June 1745, is official understatement of the most ludicrous kind:

> The Town Council of Edinburgh have preferred Mr. William Cleghorn to the Office of Professor of Moral Philosophy in their University, vacant by the Resignation of Dr. John Pringle, lately promoted Physician to his Royal Highness the Duke of Cumberland, and Physician-General to the Hospitals of his Majesty's Forces in Flanders.

Hume, himself, never expressed, so far as is known, his opinion of the man the Town Council actually chose. One member of the Hume circle, however, Adam Ferguson, who later held the professorship (1764–85), saw enough merit in Cleghorn to make him participate with Hume in an imaginary conversation, a 'Dialogue on a Highland Jaunt'. The other speakers are William Wilkie, poet and professor; Robert Adam, the architect; and Ferguson himself. Cleghorn is presented as agreeing with Ferguson and opposing Hume, and this might suggest that in the eyes of contemporaries they were worthy opponents for the chair. Unfortunately, Cleghorn had not published anything by the time of his early death at thirty-five.[10]

Hume made one further attempt, half-heartedly, to secure an academic post, that of Professor of Logic in Glasgow University, 1751–2. Adam Smith, Professor of Moral Philosophy, friend and admirer of Hume, remarked laconically: 'I should prefer David Hume to any man for a colleague; but I am afraid the public would not be of my opinion; and the interest of the society will oblige us to have some regard to the opinion of the Public'.[11] Had Hume actually forgotten, or deliberately disregarded, his own realistic sentiments of 1739 expressed to Professor Hutcheson? 'Except a Man be in Orders, or be immediately concern'd in the Instruction of Youth', he had observed,

'I do not think his Character depends upon his philosophical Speculations, as the World is now model'd . . .' (*H L*, I, 34). Speculation as to what might have happened had Hume actually received an academic appointment is perhaps inevitable; also inevitable is the conclusion that he would have been in hot water from the start—there are always High-Flyers, always politicians, always the gullible public. In the brief autobiography written shortly before his death, Hume made no mention of his abortive academic career.

VII. *A Letter from a Gentleman* (1745), like *An Abstract of a Treatise of Human Nature* (1740), is concerned with Hume's defence of his philosophical principles against abusive and invidious attack. Both are written in the third person and both bear incontestably the mark of Hume's thought and style. The one thing that he genuinely regretted about the *Treatise*, stated time and time again over the course of a lifetime, was its too hasty publication. As he put it at the close of *A Letter from a Gentleman*: 'I am indeed of Opinion, that the Author had better delayed the publishing of that Book; not on account of any dangerous Principles contained in it, but because on more mature Consideration he might have rendered it much less imperfect by further Corrections and Revisals'. The fact is that in 1745 Hume was already regretting, not the arguments of the *Treatise* but the *tone* of their presentation. He was, indeed, recasting his first book: thus Weldehall was the birthplace not only of *A Letter from A Gentleman* (1745) but also of *Philosophical Essays concerning Human Understanding* (1748). The years 1746–8 were occupied with Hume's military and diplomatic adventures with General St Clair.

The *Abstract*, at least in the form in which it has survived and been reprinted in 1938 by J. M. Keynes and P. Sraffa (and again by offset process in 1965) is a concise, reasoned and lucid explication of the main argument, that is, causality, of the first book of the *Treatise*. Its full title runs: *An Abstract of a Book lately Published; Entituled, A Treatise of Human Nature, &c. Wherein The Chief Argument of that Book is farther Illustrated and Explained.* However, an earlier title was announced in the *Daily Advertiser* of 11 March 1740: *An Abstract of a late Philosophical Performance, entitled A Treatise of Human Nature, &c. Wherein the chief Argument and Design of that Book, which has met with such Opposition, and been represented in so Terrifying a Light, is further illustrated and explain'd.* This title is emotionally coloured, but it is idle to speculate whether in some earlier version the text itself was equally charged. In its extant form, the *Abstract* was a considered effort, at least the third over the course of several months, to summarize basic philosophical concepts.

In contrast, *A Letter from a Gentleman*, according to its author, was 'composed in one Morning'. Is this likely, to compose approximately 7,500 words in one morning? Probably not, but is Hume's statement, then, totally unacceptable? No, since the first half of *A Letter from a Gentleman* is direct quotation, Hume, himself, composed only the second half, which is quite possible, though it is certainly fast composition.

A Letter from a Gentleman is more personal in tone than the *Abstract* because Hume is defending his qualifications for a professorship. Specifically, he is setting himself up to refute six charges brought against him (17-18). The charges are: (1) 'Universal Scepticism', (2) 'Principles leading to downright Atheism, by denying the Doctrine of Causes and Effects', (3) 'Errors concerning the very Being and Existence of a God', (4) 'Errors concerning God's being the first Cause, and prime Mover of the Universe', (5) 'denying the Immateriality of the Soul, and the Consequences flowing from this Denial', and (6) 'sapping the Foundations of Morality, by denying the natural and essential Differences betwixt Right and Wrong, Good and Evil, Justice and Injustice; making the Differences only artificial, and to arise from human Conventions and Compacts'. This last charge, based on Book III of the *Treatise*,

'Of Morals', is, of course, one that the earlier *Abstract* could not have dealt with.

Hume's reply to the six charges is valuable in a number of ways, not the least of which is that, not having a copy of the *Treatise* at hand, he was compelled to resort to memory and to reason in 1745, as it were, rather than 1739–40. Thus his views on scepticism, causality and morality are stated afresh in accounts as clear and forthright as they are concise. His rejection of the a priori in the realm of matters of fact is vigorously put and his 'common sense' and 'orthodox' attitude is emphasized. The assertion that, with the rejection of the a priori, 'all the solid Arguments for Natural Religion retain their full Force upon the Author's Principles concerning Causes and Effects' (24) might strike the learned modern reader as philosophically disingenuous. Yet the case against the a posteriori argument for the being and attributes of God was not to be fully developed and expressed by Hume until the *Dialogues concerning Natural Religion*, a work which was held in abeyance from the time of first composition in the early 1750s until posthumous publication in 1779. The last sentence of *A Letter from a Gentleman* pleads the advantage of the 'Gentleman' over the 'Opposers' of '*Innocence*', and also of '*Favour*', that is, 'if we really live in a Country of Freedom, where Informers and Inquisitors are so deservedly held in universal Detestation, where Liberty, at least of Philosophy, is so highly valu'd and esteem'd'.

Another general virtue of Hume's reply to the charges is that it augments what (in the mode of seventeenth and eighteenth-century philosophizing) had been rather neglected in the *Treatise*, though somewhat developed in the *Abstract*: the naming of names and the placing of the author in past and contemporary contexts. For example, in addition to the usual run of the Ancients, the Moderns instanced in *A Letter from a Gentleman* include Descartes, *Huet* and Malebranche of France, and Berkeley, *Clarke*, *Cudworth*, Hutcheson, Locke, *Newton*, *Tillotson* and Wollaston of Britain. The italicized names among the philosophical and theological writers of the seventeenth and eighteenth centuries are not mentioned nor alluded to in either the *Treatise* or the *Abstract*.

VIII. The editors of the reprint of the *Abstract* announced on their title-page in 1938 that they were presenting 'A Pamphlet hitherto unknown by David Hume'. Once again a 'hitherto unknown' pamphlet has come to light, though the fact that Hume had written it was disclosed in 1954 in both *The Life of David Hume* and *New Letters of David Hume*. In December 1966, the National Library of Scotland acquired its copy from a Birmingham bookseller. Its provenance has been traced to the library of Mr Johnston-Smith, Harmony Hill, Lisburn, near Belfast; how it got there remains inscrutable. The evidence of the type and ornaments, such as it is worth, suggests that the pamphlet was printed by T. Lumisden and J. Robertson of Edinburgh. The 'Pinted in the Year M. DCC. XLV', together with rather more than a half-dozen typographical errors, is indication of the haste with which it was rushed into print.

That it failed to achieve its immediate purpose need not obviate its value to posterity, a posterity that in the twentieth century has finally begun to see Hume as he intended to be seen over two hundred years ago.

A
LETTER

FROM A
GENTLEMAN
TO
His FRIEND in *Edinburgh*:

CONTAINING
Some OBSERVATIONS
ON

A Specimen of the Principles concerning
RELIGION and **MORALITY**,
said to be maintain'd in a Book lately publish'd, intituled, *A Treatise of Human
Nature*, &c.

EDINBURGH,
Pinted in the Year M. DCC. XLV.

SIR,

I Have read over the Specimen of the Principles concerning Religion and Morality, said to be maintain'd in a Book lately publifhed, intituled, *A Treatife of Human Nature*; being an Attempt to introduce the Experimental Method of Reafoning into Moral Subjects. I have alfo read over what is called *the Sum of the Charge.* Which Papers, as you inform me, have been induftriously fpread about, and were put into your Hands fome few Days ago.

I was perfwaded that the Clamour of *Scepticifm, Atheifm,* &c. had been fo often employ'd by the worft of Men againft the beft, that it had now loft all its Influence; and fhould never have thought of making any Remarks on thefe *maim'd Excerpts*, if you had not laid your Commands on me, as a Piece of common Juftice to the Author, and for undeceiving fome well-meaning People, on whom it feems the enormous Charge has made Impreffion.

A 2

I

I fhall infert the Accufation at full
Length, and then go regularly through
what is called the *Sum of the Charge*; be-
caufe it is intended, I fuppofe, to contain
the Subftance of the whole. I fhall alfo
take notice of the *Specimen* as I go along.

Specimen of the Principles concerning Religion *and* Morality, *&c.*

THE Author puts on his Title-page
(Vol. 1. printed for *J. Noon*, 1739.)
a Paffage of *Tacitus* to this Purpofe; " Rare
" Happinefs of our Times, that you may
" think as you will, and fpeak as you
" think."

He expreffes his Deference to the Publick in thefe Words (Advertifement, *p.* 2.)
" The Approbation of the Publick I con-
" fider as the *greateft* Reward of my La-
" bours; but am determined to regard its
" Judgment, *whatever it be*, as my *beft* In-
" ftruction."

458.   He gives us the fummary View of his
459. Philofophy from *p.* 458. to 470.—" I am
" confounded with that forlorn Solitude,
" in which I am placed in my Philofophy.
" —I

" —I have expofed myfelf to the Enmity
" of all Metaphyficians, Logicians, Ma-
" thematicians, and even Theologians.—
" I have declared my Difapprobations of
" their Syftems.—When I turn my Eye
" inward, I find nothing but Doubt and
" Ignorance. All the World confpires to
" oppofe and contradict me; tho' fuch is
" my Weaknefs, that I feel all !my Opi-
" nions loofen and fall of themfelves, when
" unfupported by the Approbation of
" others.—Can I be fure, that, in leaving 460.
" all eftablifhed Opinions, I am following
" Truth? and by what Criterion fhall I
" diftinguifh her, even if *Fortune* fhould
" at laft guide me on her Footfteps? After
" the moft accurate and exact of my Rea-
" fonings, I can give no Reafon why I
" fhould affent to it; and feel nothing but
" a ftrong Propenfity to confider Objects
" ftrongly in that View under which they
" appear to me.—The Memory, Senfes, 461.
" and Underftanding, are all of them foun-
" ded on the *Imagination.*—No Wonder
" a Principle fo inconftant and fallacious
" fhould lead us into Errors, when impli-
" citely followed (as it muft be) in all its
" Variations.— I have already fhown, that 464.
" the Underftanding, when it acts alone,
" and according to its moft general Princi-
" ples, *entirely* fubverts itfelf, and leaves
" not

C

" not the *lowest Degree* of Evidence in
" any Propofition either in Philofophy or
465. " common Life.— We have no Choice left,
466. " but betwixt a *falfe Reafon* and *none at*
467. " *all.*—Where am I, or what? From what
" Caufes do I derive my Exiftence, and to
" what Condition fhall I return? Whofe
" Favour fhall I court, and whofe Anger
" muft I dread? What Beings furround
" me? On whom have I any Influence, or
" who have any Influence on me? I am
" confounded with all thefe Queftions, and
" begin to fancy myfelf in the moft deplo-
" rable Condition imaginable, invironed
" with the deepeft Darknefs, and utterly
" deprived of the Ufe of every Member
468. " and Faculty.— If I muft be *a Fool*, as all
" thofe who reafon or believe any Thing cer-
" tainly are, my Follies fhall at leaft be
469. " natural and agreeable.— In all the Inci-
" dents of Life, we ought ftill to preferve
" our Scepticifm: If we believe that *Fire*
" *warms*, or *Water refrefhes*, 'tis only be-
" caufe it cofts us *too much Pains* to think
" otherwife; nay, if we are Philofophers,
" *it ought only* to be upon fceptical Princi-
470. " ples.— I cannot forbear having a Curio-
" fity to be acquainted with the Principles
" of moral Good and Evil, *&c.* I am con-
" cerned for the Condition of the *learned*
" *World*, which lies under fuch a deplo-
" rabl e

" rable Ignorance in all thefe Particulars.
" I feel an Ambition arife in me of contri-
" buting to the Inftruction of Mankind,
" and of acquiring *a Name by my Inventions*
" *and Difcoveries.*— Should I endeavour
" to banifh thefe Sentiments, I feel I
" fhould be a Lofer in point of Pleafure;
" and this is the Origin of my Philofo-
" phy."

Agreeable to this fummary View, he
tells us, *p.* 123. " Let us fix our Attention
" *out of ourfelves* as much as poffible.—
" We really never advance a Step *beyond*
" *ourfelves*; nor can conceive any Kind of
" Exiftence, but thefe Perceptions which
" have appeared in that narrow Compafs:
" This is the Univerfe of the Imagination,
" nor have we any Idea but what is there
" produced."— Accordingly, " An Opi-
" nion or Belief may be moft accurately
" defined, *A lively Idea related or affociat-* 172.
" *ed with a prefent Impreffion*; and is more 321.
" properly an Act of the fenfitive than of
" the cogitive Part of our Natures." And,
" Belief in general confifts in nothing but 363.
" the Vivacity of an Idea. Again, the Idea 122.
" of *Exiftence* is the very fame with the Idea
" of what we conceive to be exiftent. —
" Any Idea we pleafe to form is the Idea of
" a Being; and the Idea of a Being is any
" Idea we pleafe to form. And as to the
                                    " No-

" Notion of an external Exiſtence, when
" taken for ſomething ſpecifically different
" from our Perceptions, we have ſhown its
330. " Abſurdity: And what we call a Mind
" is nothing but a Heap or Collection of
" different Perceptions united together by
" certain Relations, and ſuppoſed, tho' falſ-
361. " ly, to be endowed with a perfect Simpli-
370. " city." And, " The only Exiſtence, of
" which we are certain, are Perceptions.
438. " When I enter moſt intimately into what
" I call *myſelf*, I always ſtumble on ſome
" particular Perception or other. — I never
" can catch *myſelf* at any Time without a
" Perception, and never can obſerve *any*
439. " *Thing but the Perception*. — If any one
" think he has a different Notion of him-
" ſelf, I muſt confeſs I can reaſon no long-
" er with him. — I may venture to affirm
" of the reſt of Mankind, that they are
" nothing but a Bundle of Perceptions,
" which ſucceed each other with an incon-
" ceivable Rapidity, and are in a perpetual
" Flux and Movement." — And left the
Reader ſhould forget to apply all this to
the Supreme Mind, and the Exiſtence of
the Firſt Cauſe, he has a long Diſquiſition
concerning *Cauſes* and *Effects*, the Sum of
321. which amounts to this, That all our Rea-
138. ſoning concerning Cauſes and Effects are
derived from *nothing* but *Cuſtom*: That,
" if

" if any pretend to define a Cause by saying
" it is something productive of another,
" 'tis evident he would say nothing; for
" what does he mean by Production? That 298.
" we may define a Cause to be *an Object*
" *precedent and contiguous to another, and*
" *where all the Objects resembling the for-*
" *mer are placed in like Relations of Pre-*
" *cedency and Contiguity to these Objects*
" *that resemble the latter;* or, a *Cause is*
" *an Object precedent and contiguous to ano-*
" *ther, and so united with it, that the Idea*
" *of the one determines the Mind to form*
" *the Idea of the other, and the Impression*
" *of the one to form a more lively Idea of the*
" *other."* From these clear and plain Definitions he infers, " That all Causes are of the
" same Kind; and there is no Foundation for
" the Distinction betwixt efficient Causes,
" and Causes *sine qua non*; or betwixt *efficient*
" Causes, and formal and material, and ex-
" emplary, and final Causes: And that 300.
" there is but one Kind of Necessity, and
" the common Distinction betwixt Moral 301.
" and Physical is without any Foundation
" in Nature: And that the Distinction we
" often make betwixt Power, and the Exer-
" cife of it, is equally without Foundation:
" And that the Necessity of a Cause to
" every Beginning of Existence, is not
" founded on any Arguments demonstrative

B   " or

" or intuitive: And in fine, That *any*
" *Thing* may produce *any Thing*; Creation,
" Annihilation, Motion, Reason, Volition;
" all these may arise from one another, or
" from any other Object we can imagine."
This curious *Nostrum* he often repeats,
284. *p.* 430, 434. Again he tells us, " That
" when we talk of any Being, whether of
" a Superior or Inferior Nature, as en-
" dowed with a Power or Force proportio-
" ned to any Effect,— We have really no
" distinct Meaning, and make Use only of
" common Words, without any clear and
294. " determinate Ideas. And if we have
" really no Idea of Power or Efficacy in
" any Object, or of any real Connection
" betwixt Causes and Effects, 'twill be to
" little Purpose to prove that an Efficacy
" is necessary in all Operations. We do
" not understand our own Meaning in talk-
" ing so, but ignorantly confound Ideas
" which are intirely distinct from each
291. " other." Again he says, " The Efficacy
" or Energy of Causes is neither placed in
" the Causes themselves, nor in the Deity,
" nor in the Concurrence of these two
" Principles, but belongs entirely to the
" Soul (*or the Bundle of Perceptions*)
" which considers the Union of two or
" more Objects in all past Instances : 'Tis
" here that the real Power of Causes *is*
" placed,

" placed, along with their Connection and
" Neceffity. And in fine, we may obferve
" a Conjunction or a Relation of Caufe *and*
" *Effect between different Perceptions*, but
" can never obferve it between Perceptions
" and Objects." 'Tis impoffible therefore,
that, from the Exiftence or any of the Qualities of the former, we can ever form any
Conclufion concerning the Exiftence of the
latter, or ever fatisfy our Reafon in this
Particular with regard to the Exiftence of a
Supreme Being. 'Tis well known that this
Principle, *Whatever begins to exift muft
have a Caufe of Exiftence*, is the firft Step
in the Argument for the Being of a Supreme Caufe; and that, without it, 'tis impoffible to go one Step further in that Argument. Now this Maxim he is at great
Pains from *p.* 141. to explode, and to fhow,
" That it is neither intuitively nor demon-
" ftratively certain;" and he fays, " Reafon
" can never fatisfy us that the Exiftence of
" any Object does ever imply that of
" another. So that, when we pafs from 173.
" the Impreffion of one to the Idea and
" Belief of another, we are not determined
" by Reafon, but by Cuftom." In a mar- 172.
ginal Note on the preceeding Page he fays,
" In that Propofition, *God is*, or indeed
" any other which regards Exiftence, the
" Idea of Exiftence is no diftinct Idea

" which

" which we unite with that of the Ob-
" ject, and which is capable of forming a
" compound Idea by the Union." Con-
280. cerning this Principle, *That the Deity is*
the prime Mover of the Univerſe, who firſt
created Matter, and gave its original Im-
pulſe, and likewiſe ſupports its Exiſtence,
and ſucceſſively beſtows on it its Motions;
he ſays, " This Opinion is certainly very
" curious, but it will appear ſuperfluous to
" examine it in this Place.— For, if the
" very Idea be derived from an Impreſſion,
" the Idea of a Deity proceeds from the
" ſame Origin ; and, if no Impreſſion im-
" plies any Force or Efficacy, 'tis equally
" impoſſible to diſcover, or even imagine,
" any ſuch active Principle in the Deity.
" — Since Philoſophers therefore have con-
" cluded, that Matter cannot be endowed
" with any efficacious Principle, becauſe it
" is impoſſible to diſcover in it ſuch a
" Principle ; the ſame Courſe of Reaſon-
" ing ſhould determine them to exclude it
" from the Supreme Being : Or if they
" eſteem that Opinion abſurd and impi-
" ous, as it really is, I ſhall tell them how
" they may avoid it, and that is, by *con-*
" *cluding from the very firſt*, that they
" have no adequate Idea of Power or Effi-
" cacy in any Object ; ſince neither in
" Body nor Spirit, neither in Superior nor
" In-

" Inferior Natures, are they able to dif-
" cover one fingle Inftance of it." And
fays he, " We have no Idea of a Being 432.
" endowed with any Power, much lefs of
" one endowed with infinite Power."

Concerning *the Immateriality of the
Soul* (from which the Argument is taken
for its natural Immortality, or that it cannot perifh by Diffolution as the Body) he
fays, " We certainly may conclude that 431.
" Motion may be and actually is the Caufe of
" Thought and Perception : And no won- 434.
" der, for any Thing may be the Caufe or
" Effect of *any Thing* ; which evidently
" gives the Advantage to the Materialifts
" above their Adverfaries." But yet more 418.
plainly, " I affert, fays he, that the Do-
" ctrine of the Immateriality, Simplicity,
" and Indivifibility of a thinking Subftance,
" *is a true Atheifm*, and will ferve to jufti-
" fy *all* thefe Sentiments for which *Spinoza*
" is fo univerfally infamous." This hideous 419.
Hypothefis is almoft the fame with that of
the Immateriality of the Soul, which has
become fo popular. And again he endea- 423.
vours to prove, that all the Abfurdities
which have been found in the Syftems of
Spinoza, may likewife be difcovered in that
of the Theologians : And concludes, that 425.
" We cannot advance one Step towards the
" eftablifhing the Simplicity and Immateri-
" ality

" ality of the Soul, without preparing the
" Way for a dangerous and irrecoverable
" Atheifm."

The Author's Sentiments in Morality we
have in Vol. 3. printed for *T. Longman*,
p. 5. 1740. He there tells us, that " Reafon
" has no Influence on our Paffions and
" Actions: Actions may be laudable or
" blameable, but they cannot be *reafonable*
19. " or *unreafonable.* That all Beings in the
" Univerfe, confidered in themfelves, ap-
" pear entirely loofe and independent of
" each other; 'Tis only by Experience we
" learn their Influence and Connection,
" and this Influence we ought *never* to
" extend beyond *Experience.*"

He takes great Pains to prove, from
p. 37. That Juftice is not a natural, but an
artificial Virtue; and gives one pretty odd
128. Reafon for it: " We may conclude, that
" the Laws of Juftice, being univerfal and
" perfectly inflexible, can never be derived
101. " from Nature. I fuppofe (fays he) a
" Perfon to have lent me a Sum of Money,
" on Condition that it be reftored in a few
" Days; and alfo fuppofe, that, after Ex-
" piration of the Term agreed on, he de-
" mands the Sum: I ask, *What Reafon or*
43. " *Motive have I to reftore the Money?* Pub-
" lickIntereft is not naturally attatch'd to the
" Obfervation of the Rules of Juftice, but
" is

" is only connected with it, after an artifi- 48.
" cial Convention, for the Eftablifhment
" of thefe Rules. Unlefs we will allow that
" Nature has eftablifhed a *Sophiftry*, and
" rendered it neceffary and unavoidable;
" we muft allow that the Senfe of Juftice
" and Injuftice is not derived from Nature,
" but arifes artificially, tho' neceffarily,
" from Education and human Conventions. 69.
" Here is a Propofition which I think may
" be regarded as certain, *That it is only*
" *from the Selfifhnefs and confined Genero-*
" *fity of Men, along with the fcanty Pro-*
" *vifion Nature has made for his Wants,*
" *that Juftice derives its Origin.* Thefe
" Impreffions, which give Rife to this
" Senfe of Juftice, are not natural to
" the Mind of Man, but arife from Arti-
" fice and human Conventions. Without 734.
" fuch a Convention, no one would ever
" have dreamed that there was fuch a Vir-
" tue as Juftice, or have been induced to
" conform his Actions to it. Taking
" any fingle Act, my Juftice may be per-
" nicious in every Refpect: And 'tis only
" upon the Suppofition that others are to
" imitate my Example, that I can be in-
" duced to embrace that Virtue; fince no-
" thing but the Combination can render
" Juftice advantageous, or afford me any
" Motive to conform myfelf to its Rules.
                                    " And

44. " And in general it may be affirmed, that
" there is no such Passion in human Minds,
" *as the Love of Mankind* merely as such,
" independent of personal Qualities, of
" Service or of Relation to ourself."

Mr. *Hobbs*, who was at Pains to shake
loose all other natural Obligations, yet
found it necessary to leave, or pretended to
leave, the Obligation of Promises or Pacti-
ons; but our Author strikes a bolder Stroke:

101. " That the Rule of Morality (says he)
" which enjoins the Performance of *Pro-*
" *mises*, is not natural, will sufficiently ap-
" pear from these two Propositions, which
" I proceed to prove, *viz. That a Promise*
" *would not be intelligible before human*
" *Conventions had established it*; and that,

114. " *even if it were intelligible, it would not*
" *be attended with any moral Obligation.*"
And he concludes, " That Promises im-
" pose no natural Obligation." And, *p.* 115.
" I shall further observe, That since every
" new Promise imposes a new Obligation
" of Morality upon the Person who pro-
" mises, and since this new Obligation
" arises from his Will, it is one of the
" most mysterious and incomprehensible
" Operations that can possibly be imagi-
" ned, and may even be compared to
" Transubstantiation or *Holy Orders*, where
" a certain Form of Words, along with a
" cer-

" certain Intention, changes entirely the
" Nature of an external Object, and even
" of a human Creature. In fine (fays 117.
" he) as Force is fuppofed to invalidate all
" Contracts, fuch a Principle is a Proof
" that Promifes have no natural Obliga-
" tion, and are mere artificial Contrivances,
" for the Conveniency and Advantage of
" Society."

Sum of the Charge.

From the preceeding Specimen it will
appear, that the Author maintains,

1. Univerfal Scepticifm. See his Afferti-
ons, *p.* 458,— 470. where he doubts of
every Thing (his own Exiftence excepted)
and maintains the Folly of pretending to
believe any Thing with Certainty.

2. Principles leading to downright Atheifm, by denying the Doctrine of Caufes and
Effects, *p.* 321, 138, 298, 300, 301, 303,
430, 434, 284. where he maintains, that the
Neceffity of a Caufe to every Beginning of
Exiftence is not founded on any Arguments
demonftrative or intuitive.

3. Errors concerning the very Being and
Exiftence of a God. For Inftance, Mar-
ginal Note, *p.* 172. as to that Propofition,
God is, he fays (or indeed as to any other
Thing which regards Exiftence) " The Idea
C   " of

" of Exiſtence is no diſtinct Idea which
" we unite with that of the Object, and
" which is capable of forming a compound
" Idea by Union."

4. Errors concerning God's being the firſt
Cauſe, and prime Mover of the Univerſe:
For as to this Principle, That the Deity firſt
created Matter, and gave it its original Im-
pulſe, and likewiſe ſupports its Exiſtence,
he ſays, "This Opinion is certainly very
" curious, but it will appear ſuperfluous
" to examine it in this Place, &c." p. 280.

5. He is chargable with denying the Immateriality of the Soul, and the Conſe-
quences flowing from this Denial, p. 431,
4, 418, 419, 423.

6. With ſapping the Foundations of Morality, by denying the natural and eſſential
Difference betwixt Right and Wrong, Good
and Evil, Juſtice and Injuſtice ; making the
Difference only artificial, and to ariſe from
human Conventions and Compacts, Vol. 2.
p. 5, 19, 128, 41, 43, 48, 69, 70, 73,
4, 44.

You ſee, *Dear Sir*, that I have concealed
no Part of the Accuſation, but have in-
ſerted the *Specimen* and *Charge*, as tranſ-
mitted to me, without the ſmalleſt Varia-
tion. I ſhall now go regularly thro' what
is called the *Sum of the Charge*, becauſe it
is

is intended, I suppose, to contain the Substance of the whole ; and shall take Notice of the *Specimen* as I go along.

1*st*, As to the *Sceptecism* with which the Author is charged, I must observe, that the Doctrine of the *Pyrrhonians* or *Scepticks* have been regarded in all Ages as Principles of mere Curiosity, or a Kind of *Jeux d' esprit*, without any Influence on a Man's steady Principles or Conduct in Life. In Reality, a Philosopher who affects to doubt of the Maxims of *common Reason*, and even of his *Senses*, declares sufficiently that he is not in earnest, and that he intends not to advance an Opinion which he would recommend as Standards of Judgment and Action. All he means by these Scruples is to abate the Pride of *mere human Reasoners*, by showing them, that even with regard to Principles which seem the clearest, and which they are necessitated from the strongest Instincts of Nature to embrace, they are not able to attain a full Consistence and absolute Certainty. *Modesty* then, and *Humility*, with regard to the Operations of our natural Faculties, is the Result of *Scepticism* ; not an universal Doubt, which it is impossible for any Man to support, and which the first and most trivial Accident in Life must immediately disconcert and destroy.

How

How is such a Frame of Mind prejudicial to Piety? And must not a Man be ridiculous to assert that our Author denies the Principles of Religion, when he looks upon them as equally certain with the Objects of his Senses? If I be as much assured of these Principles, as that this Table at which I now write is before me; Can any Thing further be desired by the most rigorous Antagonist? 'Tis evident, that so extravagant a Doubt as that which Scepticism may seem to recommend, by destroying *every Thing*, really affects *nothing*, and was never intended to be understood *seriously*, but was meant as a *mere* Philosophical Amusement, or Trial of *Wit* and *Subtilty*

This is a Construction suggested by the very Nature of the Subject; but he has not been contented with that, but expresly declared it. And all those Principles, cited in the *Specimen* as Proofs of his Scepticism, are positively renounced in a few Pages afterwards, and called the Effects of *Philosophical Melancholy* and *Delusion*. These are his very Words; and his Accuser's overlooking them may be thought very prudent, but is a Degree of Unfairness which appears to me altogether astonishing.

Were Authorities proper to be employed in any Philosophical Reasoning, I could cite you that of *Socrates* the wisest and

most

moſt religious of the *Greek* Philoſophers, as well as *Cicero* among the *Romans*, who both of them carried their Philoſophical Doubts to the higheſt Degree of Scepticiſm. All the antient Fathers, as well as our firſt Reformers, are copious in repreſenting the Weakneſs and Uncertainty of *mere* human Reaſon. And Monſieur *Huet* the learned Biſhop of *Avaranches* (ſo celebrated for his *Demonſtration Evangelique* which contains all the great Proofs of the Chriſtian Religion) wrote alſo a Book on this very Topick, wherein he endeavours to revive all the Doctrines of the antient *Scepticks* or *Pyrrhonians.*

In Reality, whence come all the various Tribes of Hereticks, the *Arians, Socinians* and *Deiſts*, but from too great a Confidence in mere human Reaſon, which they regard as the *Standard* of every Thing, and which they will not ſubmit to the ſuperior Light of Revelation? And can one do a more eſſential Service to Piety, than by ſhowing them that this boaſted Reaſon of theirs, ſo far from accounting for the great Myſteries of the Trinity and Incarnation, is not able fully to ſatisfy itſelf with regard to its own Operations, and muſt in ſome Meaſure fall into a Kind of implicite Faith, even in the moſt obvious and familiar Principles?

II. The Author is charged with Opinions

D

ons leading to *downright Atheism*, chiefly by denying this Principle, *That whatever begins to exist must have a Cause of Existence.* To give you a Notion of the Extravagance of this Charge, I must enter into a little Detail. It is common for Philosophers to distinguish the Kinds of Evidence into *intuitive, demonstrative, sensible*, and *moral*; by which they intend *only* to mark a Difference betwixt them, not to denote a Superiority of one above another. *Moral Certainty* may reach as *high* a Degree of Assurance as *Mathematical*; and our Senses are surely to be comprised amongst the clearest and most convincing of all Evidences. Now, it being the Author's Purpose, in the Pages cited in the Specimen, to examine the Grounds of that Proposition; he used the Freedom of disputing the common Opinion, that it was founded on *demonstrative* or *intuitive Certainty*; but asserts, that it is supported by *moral Evidence*, and is followed by a Conviction of the same Kind with these Truths, *That all Men must die*, and that *the Sun will rise To-morrow.* Is this any Thing like denying the Truth of that Proposition, which indeed *a Man must have lost all common Sense to doubt of?*

But, granting that he had denied it, how is this a Principle that leads to Atheism?

It

It would be no difficult Matter to show, that the Arguments *a posteriori* from the Order and Course of Nature, these Arguments so sensible, so convincing, and so obvious, remain still in their full Force; and that nothing is affected by it but the *metaphysical*Argument *a priori*, which many Men of Learning cannot comprehend, and which many Men both of Piety and Learning show no great Value for. Bishop *Tillotson* has used a Degree of Freedom on this Head, which I would not willingly allow myself; 'tis in his excellent Sermon *concerning the Wisdom of being religious*, where he says, *That the Being of a God is not capable of Demonstration, but of moral Evidence.* I hope none will pretend that that pious Prelate intended by these Assertions to weaken the Evidences for a Divine Existence, but only to distinguish accurately its Species of Evidence.

I say further, that even the metaphysical Arguments for a Deity are not affected by a Denial of the Proposition above-mentioned. It is only Dr. *Clark*'s Argument which can be supposed to be any way concerned. Many other Arguments of the same Kind still remain; *Des Cartes*'s for Instance, which has always been esteemed as solid and convincing as the other. I shall add, that a great Distinction ought always to be made
made

made betwixt a Man's pofitive and avowed Opinions, and the Inferences which it may pleafe others to draw from them. Had the Author really denied the Truth of the foregoing Propofition, (which the moft fuperficial Reader cannot think ever entred his Head) ftill he could not properly be charged as defigning to invalidate any one Argument that any Philofopher has employed for a *Divine Exiftence*; that is only an Inference and Conftruction of others, which he may refufe if he thinks proper.

Thus you may judge of the Candor of the whole Charge, when you fee the affigning of *one Kind of Evidence* for a Propofition, inftead of *another*, is called denying that Propofition; that the invalidating only *one Kind* of Argument for the Divine Exiftence is called *pofitive Atheifm*; nay, that the weakning only of *one individual Argument* of that Kind is called rejecting that *whole Species of Argument*, and the Inferences of others are afcribed to the Author as his real Opinion.

'Tis impoffible ever to fatisfy a captious Adverfary, but it would be eafy for me to convince the fevereft Judge, that all the folid Arguments for Natural Religion retain their full Force upon the Author's Principles concerning Caufes and Effects, and that there is no Neceffity even for altering

tering

tering the common Methods of expressing or conceiving these Arguments. The Author has indeed asserted, That we can judge only of the Operations of Causes by Experience, and that, reasoning *a priori*, any thing might appear able to produce any thing. We could not know that Stones would descend, or Fire burn, had we not Experience of these Effects; and indeed, without such Experience, we could not certainly infer the Existence of one Thing from that of another. This is no great Paradox, but seems to have been the Opinion of several Philosophers, and seems the most obvious and familiar Sentiment on that Subject; but, tho' all Inferences concerning Matter of Fact be thus resolved into Experience, these Inferences are noway weakned by such an Assertion, but on the contrary will be found to acquire more Force, as long as Men are disposed to trust to their Experience rather than to mere human Reasoning. Wherever I see Order, I infer from Experience that *there*, there hath been Design and Contrivance. And the same Principle which leads me into this Inference, when I contemplate a Building, regular and beautiful in its whole Frame and Structure; the same Principle obliges me to infer an infinitely perfect Architect, from the infinite Art and Contrivance which is display'd in the whole

D   Fa-

Fabrick of the Univerſe. Is not this the
Light in which this Argument hath been
placed by all Writers concerning Natural
Religion ?

III. The next Proof of Atheiſm is ſo
unaccountable, that I know not what to
make of it. Our Author indeed aſſerts,
after the preſent pious and learned Biſhop
of *Cloyne*, That we have no *abſtract* or
general Ideas, properly ſo ſpeaking ; and
that thoſe Ideas, which are called general,
are nothing but particular Ideas affixed to
general Terms. Thus, when I think of a
Horſe in general, I muſt always conceive
that Horſe as black or white, fat or lean, *&c.*
and can form no Notion of a Horſe that is
not of ſome particular Colour or Size. In
Proſecution of the ſame Topick, the Author hath ſaid, That we have no general
Idea of Exiſtence, diſtinct from every particular Exiſtence. But a Man muſt have
ſtrange Sagacity, that could diſcover Atheiſm
in ſo harmleſs a Propoſition. This, in my
Opinion, might be juſtified before the
Univerſity of *Salamanca*, or a *Spaniſh* In-
quiſition. I do indeed believe, that, when
we aſſert the Exiſtence of a Deity, we do
not form a general abſtract Idea of Exiſtence, which we unite with the Idea of
God, and which is capable of forming
a compound Idea by Union ; but this is
the

the Cafe with regard to every Propofition concerning Exiftence. So that, by this Courfe of Reafoning, we muft deny the Exiftence of every Thing, even of ourfelves, of which at leaft even the Accufer himfelf will admit our Author is perfwaded.

IV. Ere anfwering the fourth Charge, I muft ufe the Freedom to deliver a fhort Hiftory of a particular Opinion in Philofophy. When Men confidered the feveral Effects and Operations of Nature, they were led to examine into the Force or Power by which they were performed ; and they divided into feveral Opinions upon this Head, according as their *other* Principles were more or lefs favourable to Religion. The Followers of *Epicurus* and *Strato* afferted, That this Force was original and inherent in Matter, and, operating blindly, produced all the various Effects which we behold. The *Platonick* and *Peripatetick* Schools, perceiving the Abfurdity of this Propofition, afcribed the Origin of all Force to one primary efficient Caufe, who firft beftowed it on Matter, and fuccefsively guided it in all its Operations. But all the antient Philofophers agreed, that there was a real Force in Matter, either original or derived ; and that it was really Fire which burnt, and Food that nourifhed, when we obferved any of thefe

Ef-

Effects to follow upon the Operations of these Bodies : The Schoolmen supposed also a real Power in Matter, to whose Operations however the continual Concurrence of the Deity was requisite, as well as to the Support of that Existence which had been bestowed on Matter, and which they considered as a perpetual Creation. No one, till *Des Cartes* and *Malbranche*, ever entertained an Opinion that Matter had no Force either *primary* or *secondary*, and *independent* or *concurrent*, and could not so much as properly be called an *Instrument* in the Hands of the Deity, to serve any of the Purposes of Providence. These Philosophers last-mentioned substituted the Notion of *occasional Causes*, by which it was asserted that a Billiard Ball did not move another by its Impulse, but was only the Occasion why the Deity, in pursuance of general Laws, bestowed Motion on the second Ball. But, tho' this Opinion be very innocent, it never gained great Credit, especially in *England*, where it was considered as too much contrary to received popular Opinions, and too little supported by Philosophical Arguments, ever to be admitted as any Thing but a *mere Hypothesis.* *Cudworth, Lock* and *Clark* make little or no mention of it. Sir *Isaac Newton* (tho' some of his Followers have taken a dif-

different Turn of thinking) plainly rejects it, by fubftituting the Hypothefis of an Ætheral Fluid, not the immediate Volition of the Deity, as the Caufe of Attraction. And, in fhort, this has been a Difpute left entirely to the Arguments of Philofophers, and in which Religion has never been fuppofed to be in the leaft concerned.

Now it is evidently concerning this *Cartefian Doctrine*, of *fecondary Caufes*, the Author is treating, when he fays, (in the Paffage referred to in the Charge) *That it was a curious Opinion, but which it would appear fuperfluous to examine in that Place.*

The Topick there handled is fomewhat abftract : But I believe any Reader will eafily perceive the Truth of this Affertion, and that the Author is far from pretending to deny (as afferted in the Charge) *God's being the firft Caufe and prime Mover of the Univerfe.* That the Author's Words could have no fuch Meaning as they ftand connected, is to me fo evident, that I could pledge on this Head, not only my fmall Credit as a Philofopher, but even all my Pretenfions to Truft or Belief in the common Affairs of Life.

V. As to the fifth Article ; The Author has not anywhere that I remember denied
the

the Immateriality of the Soul in the common Senſe of the Word. He only ſays, That that Queſtion did not admit of any diſtinct Meaning ; becauſe we had no diſtinct Idea of Subſtance. This Opinion may be found everywhere in Mr. *Lock*, as well as in Biſhop *Berkley*.

VI. I come now to the laſt Charge, which, according to the prevalent Opinion of Philoſophers in this Age, will certainly be regarded as the ſevereſt, *viz.* the Author's deſtroying all the Foundations of Morality.

He hath indeed denied the eternal Difference of Right and Wrong in the Senſe in which *Clark* and *Woolaſton* maintained them, *viz.* That the Propoſitions of Morality were of the ſame Nature with the Truths of Mathematicks and the abſtract Sciences, the Objects *merely* of Reaſon, not the *Feelings* of our internal *Taſtes* and *Sentiments*. In this Opinion he concurs with all the antient Moraliſts, as well as with Mr. *Hutchiſon* Profeſſor of Moral Philoſophy in the Univerſity of *Glaſgow*, who, with others, has revived the antient Philoſophy in this Particular. How poor the Artifice, to cite a *broken Paſſage* of a Philoſophical Diſcourſe, in order to throw an Odium on the Author !

When the Author aſſerts that Juſtice is an *artificial* not a *natural Virtue*, he ſeems
ſen-

senfible that he employed Words that admit of an invidious Confiruction; and therefore makes ufe of all proper Expedients, by *Definitions* and *Explanations*, to prevent it. But of thefe his Accufer takes no Notice. By the *natural Virtues* he plainly under-ftands *Compaffion* and *Generofity*, and fuch as we are immediately carried to by a *natural Inftinct*; and by the *artificial Virtues* he means *Juftice*, *Loyalty*, and fuch as require, along with a *natural Inftinct*, a certain Re-flection on the general Interefts of Human Society, and a Combination with others. In the fame Senfe, Sucking is an Action na-tural to Man, and Speech is artificial. But what is there in this Doctrine that can be fuppofed in the leaft pernicious? Has he not exprefly afferted, That Juftice, in another Senfe of the Word, is fo natural to Man, that no Society of Men, and even no indi-vidual Member of any Society, was ever entirely devoid of all Senfe of it? Some Perfons (tho' without any Reafon, in my Opinion) are difpleafed with Mr. *Hutchifon's* Philofophy, in founding all the Virtues fo much on *Inftinct*, and admitting fo little of *Reafon* and *Reflection*. Thofe fhould be pleafed to find that fo confiderable a Branch of the Moral Duties are founded on that Principle.

The Author has likewife taken care in

121748 pofipolitive Terms to allert, That he does not maintain that Men ly under no Obligation to obferve Contracts, independent of Society; but only, that they never would have formed Contracts, and even would not have underftood the Meaning of them, independent of Society. And whereas it is obferved in the Specimen, That our Author offers further to prove, that, fuppofe a Promife was intelligible before Human Conventions had eftablifhed it, it would not be attended with any Moral Obligation. The moft carelefs Reader muft perceive that he does not underftand *Moral* in fuch an extended Senfe, as to deny the Obligation of Promifes, independent of Society; feeing he not only afferts what is above-reprefented, but likewife that the Laws of Juftice are univerfal, and perfectly inflexible. It is evident, that fuppofe Mankind, in fome primitive unconnected State, fhould by fome Means come to the Knowledge of the Nature of thofe Things which we call Contracts and Promifes; that this Knowledge would have laid them under no fuch actual Obligation, if not placed in fuch Circumftances as give rife to thefe Contracts.

I am forry I fhould be obliged to cite from my Memory, and cannot mention Page and Chapter fo accurately as the Accufer. I came hither by Poft, and brought no

Books

Books along with me, and cannot now provide myself in the Country with the Book
referred to.

This long Letter, with which I have
troubled you, was composed in one Morning, that I might gratify your Demand of
an immediate Answer to the heavy Charge
brought against your Friend; and this, I
hope, will excuse any Inaccuracies that may
have crept into it. I am indeed of Opinion,
that the Author had better delayed the publishing of that Book; not on account
of any dangerous Principles contained in it,
but because on more mature Consideration
he might have rendered it much less imperfect by further Corrections and Revisals.
I must not at the same Time omit obser-
ving, that nothing can be wrote so accurately or innocently, which may not be perver-
ted by such Arts as have been imployed on
this Occasion. No Man would undertake
so invidious a Task as that of our Author's
Accuser, who was not actuated by particular Interests; and you know how easy it
is, by broken and partial Citations, to pervert any Discourse, much more one of so
abstract a Nature, where it is difficult, or
almost impossible, to justify one's self to the
Publick. The Words which have been
carefully pickt out from a large Volume will
no doubt have a dangerous Aspect to careless

E   Rea-

Readers; and the Author, in my Apprehension, cannot fully defend himself without a particular Detail, which it is impoffible for a carelefs Reader to enter into. This Advantage of the Ground has been trufted to by his Accufer, and furely never more abufed than on the prefent Occafion. But he has one Advantage, I truft, which is worth a Hundred of what his Oppofers can boaft of, viz. *that of Innocence*; and I hope he has alfo another Advantage, *viz. that of Favour*, if we really live in a Country of Freedom, where Informers and Inquifitors are fo defervedly held in univerfal Deteftation, where Liberty, at leaft of Philofophy, is fo highly valu'd and efteem'd. I am,

Sir,

Your moft obedient

May 8*th* 1745. *humble Servant.*

Notes to the Introduction

1. Bishop Butler is not included among 'the most prominent British philosophers of the mid-1740s' because he published no more philosophy after the *Analogy of Religion* (1736). It is not claimed, of course, that Butler and Hutcheson are in the same class as Hume and Berkeley.

2. J. Y. T. Greig (ed.) *The Letters of David Hume* I (Oxford 1932) 56. Hereafter cited in text as *HL*, with volume and page number.

3. An account of Coutts's correspondence and dealings with Pringle, based on the Town Council minutes and those of the University Senate, is provided in E. C. Mossner *The Life of David Hume* (Edinburgh and Austin 1954) 153-61. The present account, though necessarily repeating some of the former, is enriched by considerable new manuscript materials of a political nature.

4. Mark A. Thomson *The Secretaries of State,* 1681–1782 (Oxford 1932) 36.

5. This and succeeding quotations, hitherto unnoticed, from the letters of Arbuthnott and Hay to Lord Tweeddale are taken from National Library of Scotland MS. 7076 (part of the Yester Papers). References in the text give the date of the letter.

6. Raymond Klibansky and E. C. Mossner (eds.) *New Letters of David Hume* (Oxford 1954) 15.

35

Hereafter cited in text as *NHL*, with page number.

7.   GWITMARPSCHELDON, Wishart's odd-sounding pen-name, may be an anagram: M[agister] G[welmus] WISHART C[A]LEDON[ius] or [icus]. The suggestion is Professor D. B. Horn's. Professor Ian Ross submits, on the contrary, that Wishart has made up a name from a Dutch jingle possibly heard in childhood, his father being educated in part in Holland: 'Guit, maar op shelden uit' = 'Rascal [in a playful sense], but only to the user of abusive language'. The editors, for their part, remain neutral and content to remind the reader of the barker's chant at the carnival: 'You pays your money and you takes your choice'.

8.   Douglas Nobbs 'Political Ideas of William Cleghorn, Hume's Academic Rival' *Journal of the History of Ideas* XXVI, 4 (1965) 567.

9.   *The Lord Provosts of Edinburgh*, 1296–1932 (Edinburgh 1932) 66.

10.   See E. C. Mossner 'Adam Ferguson's "Dialogue on a Highland Jaunt" with Robert Adam, William Cleghorn, David Hume, and William Wilkie', in Carroll Camden (ed.) *Restoration and Eighteenth-Century Literature* (Chicago 1963) 297-308.

11.   John Thomson *Account of the Life . . . of William Cullen, M. D.* 1 (Edinburgh 1832–59) 606.

Notes to Hume's Text

p.21, l.8: Pierre Daniel Huet (1630–1721). The *Demonstratio Evangelica* appeared in 1679; the *Traité de la faiblesse de l'esprit humain* in 1723, English translation, 1725.

p.23, l.11: John Tillotson (1630–94) was made Archbishop of Canterbury in 1691. Hume is not quoting directly from Tillotson as the work was not available to him at Weldehall. Presumably the passage he had in mind is the following: '*Mathematical* things, being of an abstracted nature are capable of the clearest and strictest *Demonstration*; But Conclusions in *Natural Philosophy* are capable of proof by an *Induction* of experiments; things of a *moral* nature by *moral* arguments; and *matters of fact* by *credible testimony*. And tho none of these be capable of that strict kind of *demonstration*, which Mathematical matters are; yet have we an undoubted assurance of them, when they are proved by the best arguments that things of that kind will bear. . . . Now to apply this to the present case. The being of a God is not *Mathematically* demonstrable, nor can it be expected it should, because only Mathematical matters admit of this kind of evidence'. *The Works of John Tillotson, D.D.* (London 1707), Sermon I, 'The Wisdom of being Religious', 20–21.

37

p.23, 1.25: Samuel Clarke (1675–1729) argues in *A Discourse concerning the Being and Attributes of God, the Obligations of Natural Religion, and the Truth and Certainty of the Christian Revelation* (1705–6) that the existence of God could be demonstrated in the same way that the 'truth' of a mathematical proposition could be demonstrated.

p.23, 1.28: René Descartes (1596–1650) makes use of both the cosmological and the ontological arguments for the existence of God. Although Hume might naturally be expected to be referring to the former, in the present context he is actually referring to the latter, probably as found in the third and fifth of the *Meditationes de Primâ Philosophiâ*. In a letter of 26 August 1737, Hume had recommended this and some other books to his friend Michael Ramsay to enable him to 'easily comprehend the metaphysical Parts of my Reasoning'. See Tadeusz Kozanecki (ed.) 'Dawida Hume'a Nieznane Listy W Zbiorach Muzeum Czartoryskich (Polska)' *Archiwum Historii Filozofii I Myśli Społecznej* ix (1963) 133.

p.26, 1.8: George Berkeley (1685–1753) was made Bishop of Cloyne in 1734. Hume is referring to the *Treatise on the Principles of Human Knowledge* (1710), another of the books recommended to Ramsay.

p.28, 1.9: Nicholas Malebranche (1638–1715) was drawn to philosophical studies by reading Descartes. In *De la recherche de la vérité* (1674), he maintains the doctrine of *occasionalism*. This book was also recommended to Ramsay.

p.28, 1.18: Hume's own, and quite different, discussion of the 'Billiard Ball' appears in the *Abstract* (11-21).

p.28, 1.29: Ralph Cudworth (1617–88), author of *The True Intellectual System of the Universe* (1678) and of the posthumous *A Treatise concerning Eternal and Immutable Morality* (1731), is nowhere else mentioned in Hume's works. John Locke (1632–1704) is frequently referred to by Hume, and the yoking of

Locke with Cudworth and Clarke is clearly intended
to show how in three English philosophers the notions
of Malebranche were not seriously entertained.

p.29, 1.9: Isaac Newton (1642–1727) puts forth the
'Hypothesis of an Ætheral Fluid' in several works,
for example, in the General Scholium at the end of
Book III of the *Philosophia Naturalis Principia
Mathematica* (1687): 'a certain most subtle spirit
which pervades and lies hid in all gross bodies. . .'
(English translation of Motte, revised by Cajori
[Berkeley 1946], 547).

p.30, 1.15: William Wollaston (1660–1724). His *The
Religion of Nature Delineated* (1724) had been attacked
by Hume in a long, witty footnote in the *Treatise*
(III. i.).

p.30, 1.23: Francis Hutcheson (1694–1746). The
reference may be to *Philosophiae Moralis Institutio
Compendiaria* (1742), a copy of which Hutcheson
presented to Hume (see *H L*, I, 45); but Hume, to be
sure, was familiar with Hutcheson's earlier works.

Index of Names

© E. C. MOSSNER, J. V. PRICE AND
EDINBURGH UNIVERSITY PRESS 1967
22 George Square, Edinburgh 8
North America
Aldine Publishing Company
320 West Adams Street, Chicago
Australia and New Zealand
Hodder & Stoughton Limited
Africa, Oxford University Press
India, P. C. Manaktala & Sons
Far East, M. Graham Brash & Son

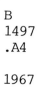